Reasoning and Writing

Level C
Workbook

Siegfried Engelmann

Jerry Silbert

A Division of The McGraw-Hill Companies

Columbus, Ohio

Cover Credits

(t) ©SuperStock, (b) Animal Graphics.

SRA/McGraw-Hill

A Division of The McGraw-Hill Companies

2008 Imprint
Copyright © 2001 by SRA/McGraw-Hill.

Send all inquires to:
SRA/McGraw-Hill
4400 Easton Commons
Columbus, OH 43219

Printed in the United States of America.

ISBN 0-02-684772-8

15 16 17 18 HES 14 13 12 11 10

Lesson 19

Part A Circle the part that names. Underline the part that tells more.

1. A horse and a goat were eating grass.
2. Those hungry animals ate all the grass.
3. They drank water from a pond.
4. A car and a truck went by a pond.
5. They were very loud.

Part B Put in capitals and periods. Circle the part of each sentence that names.

Tom and his brother went shopping for food they bought four apples and six oranges the food cost less than five dollars Tom gave the clerk five dollars the clerk gave Tom change

Part C

Mr. Walters was buying an apple tree. He dug a hole in his yard. He placed the tree in the hole. He is filling the hole with dirt. He is watering the tree. He took good care of the tree.

Do the sentences tell what Mr. Walters did? **X X X**

Part D Circle the sentence that tells the main thing each group did.

Three cowboys felt tired.

Two cowboys smiled.

The cowboys looked at the fire.

Three cowboys cooked supper.

The animals wore clothing.

The animals did tricks.

The animals were inside.

The animals got food for doing well.

Lesson 20 – Test 2

Test Score [ ]

Part A | Put in capitals and periods. Circle the part of each sentence that names.

My older sister took her dog to the park her dog chased a skunk the skunk got mad it made a terrible stink my sister had to wash her dog for hours to get rid of the smell

Part B

My friends are going to the park. They are having a good time. Two girls played on the swings. A boy chased a butterfly. A boy and a girl are running in the grass. Everybody is staying in the park until the sun went down.

Do the sentences tell what people did?   X   X   X   X

Part C | Write the letter of each picture that shows what the sentence says.

1. He held a bottle. _____

2. A person held a container. _____

3. She held a container. _____

4. He held a container. _____

Part D | Fill in the blanks with **He, She** or **It.**

1. His shirt was red and blue. _____ had stripes.

2. My mother helped me do my homework. _____ is very good at math.

3. His brother is one year old. _____ can almost walk.

Lesson  21

Put in capitals and periods. Circle the part of each sentence that names.

Sandy and her dog went for a walk they went to the park a cat ran in front of them the dog started to chase the cat the cat ran up a tree Sandy took her dog home

Part B Circle the part that names. Underline the part that tells more.

1. My best friend and my sister helped me.
2. She had two dollars.
3. My little sister was sick.
4. The horse fell over.
5. He saw a big bird next to the house.
6. A dog and a cat slept with James.

Part C In each blank, write the word that tells what somebody did.

1. gets   got
2. rides   rode
3. drinks   drank
4. teaches   taught
5. holds   held

6. rides   _____
7. teaches   _____
8. gets   _____
9. holds   _____
10. drinks   _____

Part A   Put in capitals and periods. Circle the part of each sentence that names.

A woman bought a new bike for her son it had big tires the boy liked the bike his mother showed him how to ride the bike he rode it to school his teacher let him show the bike to the class

Part B   Circle the subject. Underline the part that tells more.

1. Three older boys went to the store.
2. A horse and a dog went to a stream.
3. A man sat on a log.
4. They sat on a bench.
5. My friend and his mother were hungry.
6. My hands and my face got dirty.

Part C

Mr. Smith and his son are going to the circus. They looked at lions and tigers. A lion tamer had a whip in his hand. His whip is making a big noise. One lion is jumping through a hoop. Mr. Smith and his son are having a good time.

Does each sentence tell what someone or something did? X X X X

Part D   In each blank, write the word that tells what people did.

1. rides   _____rode_____
2. holds   _____held_____
3. teaches _____taught_____
4. drinks   _____drank_____
5. gets   _____got_____

6. teaches _____
7. holds   _____
8. gets   _____
9. rides   _____
10. drinks _____

Lesson 23

Circle the subject of each sentence. Underline the part that tells more.

1. A jet airplane made a lot of noise.

2. A man and his dog went walking.

3. He ate lunch in the office.

4. My brother and his friend played in the park.

5. A little cat drank milk.

Part B Put in capitals and periods. Circle the subject of each sentence.

Three workers built a dog house a woman nailed boards together

she used a big hammer a young man put a roof on the dog house

the workers finished the dog house in two hours

Part C In each blank, write the word that tells what somebody did.

1. drinks _____

2. holds _____

3. rides _____

4. gets _____

5. teaches _____

27

Part A   Put in the missing capitals and periods.

> every student in the class read a book. Tom and Alice read a book about animals they learned about animals that live in different parts of the world. Two students read a book about roses that book told how to take care of roses.

Part B   Circle the subject of each sentence. Underline the predicate.

1. Five cats were on the roof.
2. They read two funny books.
3. A red bird landed on a roof.
4. A dog and a cat played in their yard.
5. It stopped.

Part C   Fill in the blanks with **He, She** or **It.**

1. My grandmother loves to walk. _____ walks five miles every day.

2. Her brother is ten years old. _____ is in the fifth grade.

3. Our plane will leave at four o'clock. _____ is going to China.

Part A   Put in the missing capitals and periods.

> My class had a picnic everybody went on a bus. Our teacher brought apples and oranges. He also cooked a chicken we built a fire to cook the chicken

Part B   Change the part that names in some of the sentences to **He, She** or **It**.

ⓐ Susan loved birds. ⓑ Susan wanted to build a bird house. ⓒ Her grandfather gave Susan a book about bird houses. ⓓ Her grandfather told Susan to read it carefully. ⓔ The book was interesting. ⓕ The book showed how to build a bird house.

Part C   In each blank, write the word that tells what somebody did.

     1. holds   _____

     2. gets   _____

     3. rides   _____

     4. teaches   _____

     5. drinks   _____

Lesson 26

Part A Fix up the paragraph so each sentence begins with a capital and ends with a period.

	A little bird fell out of a tree Bill and his sister saw the little bird. it was in a pile of leaves Bill picked up the little bird his sister climbed up to the nest. Bill handed the bird to his sister she put the bird back in the nest.

Part B Next to each word, write the word that tells what somebody did.

1. thinks   <u>thought</u>
2. flies   <u>flew</u>
3. stands   <u>stood</u>
4. brings   <u>brought</u>
5. breaks   <u>broke</u>

6. stands   _____
7. brings   _____
8. thinks   _____
9. breaks   _____
10. flies   _____

Part C Change the part that names in some of the sentences to **He, She** or **It.**

ⓐ The class was playing football during recess. ⓑ Tom had the football. ⓒ Tom threw the ball as far as he could. ⓓ Alice jumped up and caught the ball. ⓔ Alice scored a touchdown. ⓕ The school bell rang. ⓖ The school bell told the class that recess was over.

Part A   Circle the subject. Underline the predicate.

1. Sara and Harry painted the kitchen blue.
2. Sara had a paintbrush.
3. Harry used a roller.
4. They stopped to eat lunch.
5. She laughed.
6. The windows were blue.

Part B   Next to each word, write the word that tells what somebody did.

1. stands   _stood_
2. thinks   _thought_
3. breaks   _broke_
4. flies   _flew_
5. brings   _brought_

6. breaks   _____
7. brings   _____
8. flies   _____
9. stands   _____
10. thinks   _____

Part C   Fix up any sentences in the paragraph that should name **He, She** or **It.**

ⓐ John wanted to have a party for his birthday. ⓑ John was going to be ten years old. ⓒ His mother planned a big party. ⓓ His mother called all John's friends. ⓔ His mother bought lots of party things. ⓕ The party started right after school. ⓖ The party was a lot of fun.

Part A   Fix up the paragraph so each sentence begins with a capital and ends with a period.

> Tom threw a rock at a tree his rock hit a beehive. the bees got very mad they flew out of the nest. Tom ran away from the bees. many bees chased him tom jumped into the lake. he never threw rocks at trees again

Part B   Circle the subject. Underline the predicate.

1. Mr. Dunn and his son went to the store.

2. Mrs. Jones met Mrs. Smith and her son.

3. Two dogs started to run around the store.

4. Mr. Jones was happy.

5. They sat in a rocking chair.

Part C   Fix up any sentences in the paragraph that should name **He, She** or **It.**

Greg cleaned up his room last week. Greg put all his toys in the closet.

His grandmother was very happy. His grandmother gave him a big hug.

Part D   Next to each word, write the word that tells what somebody did.

1. flies   _____

2. brings   _____

3. breaks   _____

4. thinks   _____

5. stands   _____

Part E

1.

2.

3.

white   black   big   small

1. A_____ cat sat on a _____ chair.

2. A_____ cat sat on a _____ chair.

3. A_____ cat sat on a _____ chair.

Part A Fix up the paragraph so each sentence begins with a capital and ends with a period.

	Snow fell all night long. Doris got up and looked outside everything was white. Doris thought about things to do in the snow she wanted to throw snowballs. She wanted to roll in the snow. her mother handed her a snow shovel. Doris went out in the snow She did not have a lot of fun

Part B Fix up any sentences in the paragraph that should name **He, She** or **It**.

Sandra wanted to play baseball. Sandra looked for her ball and bat. Her brother also wanted to play baseball. Her brother helped her look for the ball and bat. Sandra looked in the yard. Sandra found the ball and bat near the doghouse. The ball was in bad shape. The ball was all chewed up.

Part C If a word is somebody's name, begin the word with a capital letter.

nancy   he   truck   tammy   james

they   linda   ann   jack   my   sam

helen   she   window   tim   it

Part D

1.

2.

3.

| beach | tennis |

1. _____ woman held a _____ ball.

2. _____ woman held a _____ ball.

3. _____ woman held a _____ ball.

Part E   Write the word that tells what somebody did.

1. stands _____

2. breaks _____

3. thinks _____

4. brings _____

5. flies _____

Lesson 30

Part A

1.

2.

3.

seat	leg	back	arm

1. A cat sat on _____ a chair.

2. A cat sat on _____ a chair.

3. A cat sat on _____ a chair.

Part B

1. She gets a new dog.

2. His sister teached him to ride a bike.

3. The airplane flied over the mountain.

4. She standed on a table.

5. We seen an elephant at the circus.

Test 3

Test Score

Part A   Circle the subject. Underline the predicate.

1. A young man walked home.

2. It made a big noise.

3. My little sister is sick.

4. Her brother and sister went to school.

5. That pencil belongs to her.

Part B Fix up the paragraph so each sentence begins with a capital and ends with a period.

a boy threw a rock at a tree the rock missed the tree. The rock hit a beehive. The bees got mad they chased the boy. he ran all the way home

Part C Fix up any sentences that should name **He, She** or **It**.

The cooks made pizza. Tom put the pizza in the oven. Tom was very careful. Jane took the pizza out of the oven. Jane told everybody that they could eat. The pizza tasted great. The pizza had lots of cheese and tomatoes.

Part D

• An animal sat on a vehicle.   • A dog sat on a bike.   • An animal sat on a car.

1. Copy the sentence that tells about only one picture.

   _____

2. Copy the sentence that tells about two pictures.

   _____

3. Copy the sentence that tells about all the pictures.

   _____

Lesson 31

Begin all parts of a person's name with a capital letter.

1. bill jones
2. mrs. williams
3. the doctor
4. his brother

5. jill
6. sam miller
7. this boy
8. mr. adams

9. the girl
10. ted
11. the nurse
12. mrs. cash

Part B Fix up the paragraph so each sentence begins with a capital and ends with a period.

a strong wind blew down a tree and a fence a boy and a girl saw the broken fence the boy got a can of paint the girl got a hammer and nails they worked very hard to fix the fence

Part C

1. She bringed home a new dog.

2. We thinked about it all night.

3. He standed on the corner.

4. He gots new gloves for his birthday.

5. My mom teached me to ride a bike.

Part D

roof   tire   hood   trunk   headlight

1. A monkey sat on _____ a car.

2. A monkey sat on _____ a car.

3. A monkey sat on _____ a car.

Part E   Circle the subject in each sentence.   Underline the predicate.

1. That old house fell down.

2. A new flower came up in the garden.

3. She laughed at the joke.

4. The box was full of money.

5. His room was clean.

6. Three cows and two horses were in the barn.

Lesson 32

Begin all parts of a person's name with a capital letter.

1. mrs. robinson
2. her sister
3. steve crosby

4. a police officer
5. my teacher
6. tigers

7. debbie
8. mr. james
9. a clown

Part B Fill in the blanks with **He, She, It** or **They.**

1. A man and a woman ate dinner.
2. Two boys walked on the sand.
3. Our bus had a flat tire.
4. Bananas cost 68 cents.
5. The men wore red jackets.
6. That old car went fast.

1. _____ ate dinner.
2. _____ walked on the sand.
3. _____ had a flat tire.
4. _____ cost 68 cents.
5. _____ wore red jackets.
6. _____ went fast.

Part C Put in capitals and periods.

a dog ran after a cat the animals ran through the kitchen and the living room they ran up the stairs and down the stairs the dog ran slower and slower the cat kept going faster the dog stopped and fell over the cat was not even tired

Part D Rewrite the paragraph so the underlined parts give a clear picture.

An animal fell out of a large old tree. It landed on the soft ground.

A person picked it up. The person put it in a container and took it home.

40

Lesson  33

Part A   Begin all parts of a person's name with a capital letter.

1. greg
2. mrs. abbott
3. my sister
4. cowboys

5. ronnie lee
6. a little poodle
7. jerry adams
8. mr. sanders

9. cats
10. the fireman
11. peggy
12. mrs. jackson

Part B   Fill in the blanks with **He, She, It** or **They.**

1. A cow and a horse slept in the barn.
2. My shoes were wet.
3. Anna played baseball.
4. A boy shouted.
5. His sister stood in line.
6. A bottle fell off the table.

1. _____ slept in the barn.
2. _____ were wet.
3. _____ played baseball.
4. _____ shouted.
5. _____ stood in line.
6. _____ fell off the table.

Part C

A woman drove an old car she has the car for many years. She took good care of her car. She even was painting the car. Her car looked as good as new everybody likes that wonderful old car

☐ **Check 1.** Does each sentence begin with a capital and end with a period?

☐ **Check 2.** Does each sentence tell what somebody or something did?

Write **S** in front of each part that is a subject.
Write **P** in front of each part that is a predicate.

____ 1. ran to the store

____ 2. had a long tail

____ 3. my dog

____ 4. Troy and Chris

____ 5. had four new tires

____ 6. she

____ 7. my sister

____ 8. was on the table

____ 9. two dogs and three cats

____ 10. bought a yellow dress

Part E

1. He breaked his leg.

2. They rided a horse.

3. I seen my brother in the park.

4. He gots an A on the test.

5. He drinked a glass of water.

Part F Rewrite the paragraph so the underlined parts give a clear picture.

A <u>man</u> sat on <u>an object</u>. A <u>bird</u> sat on <u>him</u>. He held <u>it</u> in one hand.

He tossed <u>food</u> with the other hand. Three <u>animals</u> picked up the <u>food</u>.

Lesson 34

Part A   Write **S** in front of each part that is a subject.
Write **P** in front of each part that is a predicate.

___ 1. Jerry and Tom

___ 2. walked to the store

___ 3. played cards with Jill

___ 4. my brother and I

___ 5. three eggs

___ 6. went to the movies

___ 7. they

___ 8. she

___ 9. talked to the doctor

___10. had fun with his friend

Part B

A car went past our house. It has old tires it had four broken doors.

The car was making lots of noise smoke came out of the hood. The driver

is getting out of the car he is kicking the car his car fell apart.

☐ **Check 1.** Does each sentence begin with a capital and end with a period?

☐ **Check 2.** Does each sentence tell what somebody or something did?

Part C   Fill in the blanks with **He, She, It** or **They.**

1. Two women fixed the car.
2. My father bought a new tie.
3. The boys and girls played baseball.
4. Jill found ten dollars.
5. His bag was full of apples.
6. Those apples were not ripe.
7. Her sisters painted Jim's room.
8. David fed the dog.

1. _____ fixed the car.
2. _____ bought a new tie.
3. _____ played baseball.
4. _____ found ten dollars.
5. _____ was full of apples.
6. _____ were not ripe.
7. _____ painted Jim's room.
8. _____ fed the dog.

43

Begin all parts of a person's name with a capital letter.

1. alice
2. mr. smith
3. my brother
4. the doctor
5. the new boss
6. robert

7. mrs. adams
8. a big fish
9. a fire fighter
10. sally
11. carl sanders
12. that teacher

Part E Write **R** for each fact that is relevant.
Write **No** for each fact that is not relevant.

Question: Why did the dog bite the man?

Fact 1: The man kicked the dog before the dog bit him. _____

Fact 2: The dog had brown spots. _____

Fact 3: The man was 43 years old. _____

Fact 4: The dog hated people. _____

Part F Rewrite the paragraph so the underlined parts give a clear picture.

<u>A man</u> was carrying <u>some food</u>. He saw <u>some animals</u>. He dropped <u>it</u> and climbed up <u>a plant</u>. <u>Some of the animals</u> ate <u>it</u>. <u>Some of the animals</u> looked up at the man.

Lesson 35

Part A

James had two good friends. Their names were jill adams and robert gomez. jill and robert went to the same school that james went to. Their teacher was mr. ray.

☐ **Check.** Does each part of a person's name begin with a capital? **9**

Part B Cross out some of the names and write **He, She, It** or **They.**

Tom and Mary went to the airport. Tom and Mary were going

to meet their dad in San Francisco. Tom had never been on a

plane before. Tom was very frightened. Tom and Mary sat together

on the plane. Tom and Mary had fun after Tom stopped worrying.

Part C In each blank, write the word that tells what somebody did.

1. swims ___swam___

2. begins ___began___

3. comes ___came___

4. draws ___drew___

5. takes ___took___

6. draws _____

7. takes _____

8. begins _____

9. comes _____

10. swims _____

Write **R** for each fact that is relevant.
Write **No** for each fact that is not relevant.

Question: Why was Leon soaking wet?

Fact 1: Leon did not wear a raincoat or take an umbrella. _____

Fact 2: Leon ate breakfast with his mother and father. _____

Fact 3: It started to rain when Leon was three blocks from school. _____

Fact 4: Not many people were on the sidewalk. _____

Part E Write **S** in front of each part that is a subject.
Write **P** in front of each part that is a predicate.

___ 1. went to the circus   ___ 6. my sister

___ 2. our family   ___ 7. sat under a large tree

___ 3. laughed at the clowns   ___ 8. Tom and his sister

___ 4. was very exciting   ___ 9. ate dinner with us

___ 5. lions and tigers   ___ 10. they

Part F Rewrite the paragraph so the underlined parts give a clear picture.

She was riding a vehicle. She was in the middle of it. An animal jumped in front of it. She turned sharply. The vehicle ran into a plant. The plant damaged it.

Lesson  36

Part A   Fix up the paragraph so that none of the sentences begin with **and** or **and then.**

     Morgan threw a Frisbee to his dad. And it went over his dad's head. And then his dad ran after the Frisbee. And then he tripped in the mud. Morgan started to run after the Frisbee. And a big dog picked it up before Morgan could grab it. And then the dog ran away with it. And then Morgan chased after the dog. His dad went in the house to clean up.

Part B

1. draws   _drew_
2. swims   _swam_
3. begins   _began_
4. takes   _took_
5. comes   _came_

6. begins _____
7. comes _____
8. draws _____
9. swims _____
10. takes _____

Part C

     They cleaned the animal. She wore great big shoes and dark glasses. She squirted the animal with a hose. He wore a cowboy hat. He sat on the animal and scrubbed its back. She wore a funny suit and a tiny hat. She stood on a ladder. She poured it on the animal.

Lesson 37

Part A

      We had a good time at the park Tom played basketball with bob. Alice and jane went jogging. I listened to mr. anderson read from a book my sister went swimming we got home just in time for dinner

---

  ☐ **Check 1.** Does each sentence begin with a capital and end with a period?

  ☐ **Check 2.** Does each part of a person's name begin with a capital letter?

Part B

      Sandra went to the zoo yesterday. And then she met her friends near the monkey house. And the monkeys were doing tricks. Two monkeys were swinging by their tails. And one monkey was doing flips. And then Sandra and her friends went to the snack bar. And they bought peanuts for the monkeys.

Part C

      They were in a corral. It drove up. It started to make a loud noise. They were in it. He grabbed a rope and jumped out of it. They stayed in it.

| Part A | Circle the subject. Underline the predicate. |

1. Eddie built a fire.

2. Susan and Ellen are planning a party.

3. My old clock was broken.

4. It is very cold.

5. The horses and cows stood in the barn.

6. They gave a prize to every child.

Part B

Everybody went to the beach. And Jerry and alice built a fire on the

sand. And then Tom and bill roasted hot dogs and marshmallows. And Mr.

jones and sammy played ball.

☐ **Check 1.** Did you fix each sentence that started with **and** or **and then?**

☐ **Check 2.** Does each part of a person's name begin with a capital letter?

| Part C | Write the word that tells what somebody did. |

1. comes _____   4. takes _____

2. swims _____   5. begins _____

3. draws _____   6. thinks _____

Part A

Sam and Ellen are cooking supper for their family. Ellen made hamburgers she cooked them over a fire. Sam makes corn he was putting butter and salt on each piece. Everyone likes the meal.

☐ **Check 1.** Does each sentence begin with a capital and end with a period?

☐ **Check 2.** Does each sentence tell what somebody or something did?

Part B   Fix up the run-on sentences.

1. Two girls played football and their dad watched them and then they asked him if he wanted to play.

2. A boy asked his mother for some food and then she gave him an apple and he asked if he could also have some cheese and his mother gave him a piece of cheese.

Part C

They came out of the building.   They walked toward it.

She carried it.   He carried them.   She waved to them.

Lesson

Fix up the run-on sentences.

1. Mr. Clark went for a ride in the country and then his car ran out of gas and then he had to walk three miles to a gas station.

2. Kathy likes to read books and her favorite book was about horses and her brother gave her that book.

3. Pam's mother asked Pam to mow the lawn and then Pam started to cut the grass and it was too wet.

Test 4

Test Score ☐

Part A **Fix up each person's name so all parts of the name begin with a capital.**

1. nancy jackson   4. mr. adams   7. mrs. nelson

2. mrs. williams   5. robert smith   8. an old man

3. my father   6. her brother   9. david jordan

Part B **Fill in the blanks with He, She, It or They.**

1. Two girls ate lunch.   1. _____ ate lunch.

2. A cow and a horse slept in the barn.   2. _____ slept in the barn.

3. His sister went home.   3. _____ went home.

4. The blue pen fell off the desk.   4. _____ fell off the desk.

5. James is sick today.   5. _____ is sick today.

6. My friends went to a party.   6. _____ went to a party.

1. My little sister had fun at school.

2. They were sleeping.

3. A man and a woman walked in the park.

4. Her friend won the race.

5. She stopped working at noon.

6. My green pen cost two dollars.

Part D   Write **R** for each fact that is relevant.
Write **No** for each fact that is not relevant.

Question: Why did Linda fall asleep at school?

Fact 1: Linda's teacher made schoolwork very interesting. _____

Fact 2: Linda woke up several times last night because her baby brother was crying. _____

Fact 3: Linda liked school. _____

Fact 4: Linda had to get up an hour early in the morning. _____

Lesson 41

Part A Fill in the blanks with the correct words.

Three women worked on a house. _____ wore work clothes. _____ cut a board. _____ used a saw. _____ carried three pieces of wood. _____ carried the boards on her shoulder. _____ hammered nails into the wood.

Kay   Milly   Jean

Part B Fix up the run-on sentences.

1. Miss Wilson saw a used bike at a store and the bike was red and blue and then Miss Wilson bought it for her sister. (3)

2. Richard and his sister went to a movie and it was very funny and Richard and his sister ate popcorn and then their mother picked them up after the movie. (4)

3. Tina built a doghouse for her dog and then she looked in the doghouse and four cats were in the doghouse with her dog. (3)

Part C

1. Six bottles were on the table.

2. An old lion chased the rabbit.

3. Jane and Sue sat under a tree.

4. His brother had a candy bar.

Part D

A woman lived near our school Her name was mrs. jones she was an airplane pilot. She told us many stories about flying planes

☐ **Check 1.** Does each sentence begin with a capital and end with a period?

☐ **Check 2.** Does each part of a person's name begin with a capital letter?

Part A

1. A black pencil fell off the table.

2. My sister was sick.

3. A dog and a cat played in the park.

4. They smiled.

5. Mary sang softly.

6. An old horse drank from a bucket.

Part B   Fix up the run-on sentences in this paragraph.

Don found a lost dog and the dog had a collar around its neck. The collar had a phone number on it and then Don called the phone number and the dog's owner answered the telephone. The owner was happy that Don found the dog. He went to Don's house and then Don gave the dog to the owner.

Part C   For each verb that tells what somebody does, write the verb that tells what somebody did.

1. begins _____

2. brings _____

3. flies _____

4. swims _____

5. takes _____

6. comes _____

Part D   Fill in the blanks with the correct words.

wheelchair

_____ sat in the wheelchair.

_____ wore pajamas. The

_____ had big wheels and

little wheels. _____ had a seat, a back

and two handles. _____ held a purse.

_____ wore a skirt and a sweater.

_____ was behind the wheelchair.

_____ pushed the wheelchair.

Part A

1. She jumped into the pool.

2. A young woman read a book about dinosaurs.

3. My mother had a new car.

4. They laughed.

5. My brother and my sister ate cookies and ice cream.

Part B

Linda went on an airplane and she had never been on an airplane before. She sat in a seat next to the window and the plane took off. She fell asleep for an hour and she woke up and the plane landed. Her grandmother was waiting for her.

Part C Fill in the blanks with the correct words.

_____ and _____ worked in the garden. _____ wore work clothes. _____ dug a hole. _____ pushed the shovel down with her foot. _____ sawed a branch. _____ held the branch with one hand.

James

Alice

Part A   Fix up the run-on sentences in the paragraph.

Jessica and Mark bought a pumpkin for Halloween and the pumpkin was so big that they could not carry it home. They started to roll it home. They pushed the pumpkin up a steep hill and then Mark slipped. The pumpkin rolled down the hill. It smashed into a tree and Jessica and Mark had lots of pumpkin pie the next day.

Part B

1. walked

    was walking

2. smiled

3. picked

4. cried

Part C   Write the missing word in each item.

1. the hat that belongs to the boy   the _____**boy's**_____ hat

2. the bone that belongs to the dog   the _____ bone

3. the car that belongs to her father   her _____ car

4. the arm that belongs to the girl   the _____ arm

5. the book that belongs to my friend   my _____ book

6. the toy that belongs to the cat   the _____ toy

Part A Fix up the run-on sentences in the paragraph.

   Ronald put his finger in a bottle and his finger got stuck

in the bottle and then he asked his sister to help him. His sister got

some butter and then she rubbed the butter around the top of the

bottle. She pulled on the bottle and then his finger came out.

Part B Circle the subject. Underline the predicate. Make a **V** above every verb.

1. The boy walked to the store.

   The boy was walking to the store.

2. Two girls ate candy.

   Two girls were eating candy.

3. A fish swam in the bathtub.

   A fish was swimming in the bathtub.

Part C

1. the dress that belongs to the girl   the ___girl's___ dress

2. the tent that belongs to her friend   her _____ tent

3. the toy that belongs to my cat   my _____ toy

4. the watch that belongs to that boy   that _____ watch

5. the hammer that belongs to his mother his _____ hammer

6. the leg that belongs to my father   my _____ leg

Circle the subject. Underline the predicate. Make a V above every verb.

1. The young woman walked to the school.

   The young woman was walking to the school.

2. The children smiled at the clown.

   The children were smiling at the clown.

3. Mark and Jenny raked the leaves.

   Mark and Jenny were raking the leaves.

4. They swam in the lake.

   They were swimming in the lake.

Part B   **Fix up the run-on sentences.**

1. The boy went to the store and bought groceries.

2. The boy went to the store and then his sister bought groceries.

3. My brother mowed the lawn and swept the sidewalk.

4. My brother mowed the lawn and then he swept the sidewalk later.

5. The workers started early and their boss went home late.

6. The workers started early and went home late.

7. She ran up the stairs and went inside the house.

8. She ran up the stairs and she went inside.

Rewrite each item with an apostrophe **s.**

1. The shirt belonged to **that boy.** The shirt was red.

   _____ was red.

2. The tail belonged to **a lion.** The tail was long.

   _____ was long.

3. The desk belonged to **my teacher.** The desk was old.

   _____ was old.

4. The hand belonged to **his mother.** The hand was sore.

   _____ was sore.

5. The car belonged to **my sister.** The car was dented.

   _____ was dented.

Lesson  47

Part A Fix up the run-on sentences.

1. Melissa fed her dog and she went inside to change her shoes.

2. Ann loved horses and her big brother wanted a horse for his birthday.

3. The children went to the farm and played with the animals.

4. My brother swept the floor and washed the dishes.

5. A man and a woman watched TV and he had a sore arm.

6. Ron went to the park and fed the birds.

1. The pencil belonged to **a girl.** The pencil was yellow.

   _____ was yellow.

2. The nest belonged to **that bird.** The nest had eggs in it.

   _____ had eggs in it.

3. The glasses belonged to **my friend.** The glasses were broken.

   _____ were broken.

4. The bottle belonged to **her baby.** The bottle had milk in it.

   _____ had milk in it.

Part C Write three sentences that tell what must have happened in the middle picture. Tell about **the candle, the newspapers** and **the woman.**

bucket fell burn

Part A Fix up the run-on sentences in this paragraph.

Tom stopped in front of the pet shop and looked in the window. He saw a puppy inside and the pet store was open and Tom didn't have any money to buy the puppy. He wanted the puppy and he went home to talk to his parents. They told him he could have the puppy. Tom did jobs and then he earned the money he needed to buy the puppy

Part B Rewrite each item with an apostrophe **s.**

1. The car belonged to **Tom.** The car was new.
   _____ was new.

2. The wheel belonged to **his bike.** The wheel was bent.
   _____ was bent.

3. The motor belonged to **that truck.** The motor made a lot of noise.
   _____ made a lot of noise.

4. The finger belonged to **Sally.** The finger was swollen.
   _____ was swollen.

5. The mouth belonged to **the dog.** The mouth was sore.
   _____ was sore.

Part C   Write three sentences that tell what must have happened in the middle picture. Tell about **the horse, Bill** and **Lisa.**

1. Bill   Lisa   The horse

2.

3.

corral   grabbed   fence   rail

Lesson 49

Part A   Write four sentences that tell what must have happened in the middle picture. Tell about **the baker, the flyswatter, the pie** and **the fly.**

1.

2.

3.

pie   flyswatter   swung   flew away   splattered

Test 5

Test Score ☐

Part A Read the paragraph. Fix up any run-ons.

A turtle and a rabbit had a race and the rabbit ran very fast. The turtle could not run fast. The rabbit saw a garden full of carrots and then the rabbit stopped and ate lots of carrots. The turtle kept on running and the turtle won the race and then the rabbit got mad because he lost the race.

1. The red pencil fell on the floor. _____

2. My little brother was sleeping under the bed. _____

3. The bus had eight wheels. _____

4. My brother and my sister were running up the stairs. _____

5. They stopped. _____

6. We found a little dog. _____

1. The shirt belonged to **Tom.** The shirt was dirty.

   _____ was dirty.

2. The dog belonged to **his sister.** The dog was barking.

   _____ was barking.

3. The toy belonged to **the baby.** The toy was on the bed.

   _____ was on the bed.

4. The motor belonged to **that car.** The motor made a loud noise.

   _____ made a loud noise.

Pete Ken Al

The men went fishing. _____

were in a boat in the middle of the lake.

_____ sat in the middle of the boat.

_____ held a fishing pole in one hand

and a net in the other hand. _____

sat in the back of the boat. _____

stood in the front of the boat. _____

smiled as his fishing pole bent.

Lesson 51

Part A

1. Milly played baseball with Linda. Milly / She threw the ball.

2. Milly played baseball with Jeff. Milly / She threw the ball.

3. Gary and John went to the store. John / He had been working all day.

4. Jessica talked to Liz. Jessica / She was walking home.

5. Kathy handed a glass to Bill. Kathy / She told him where to put it.

Part B Circle all the words in column 4 that are verbs.

1	2	3	4
ran	girls	cried	went
talked	stove	bought	bird
turned	brother	house	walked
yelled	pretty	whispered	flew
sat	quietly	teacher	pretty
smiled	man	yellow	slept
fell	lazy	swam	sold

Part A

1. Tom waved to Martha. $\begin{array}{c}\text{Martha}\\\text{She}\end{array}$ was riding a horse.

2. Larry wanted to meet James. $\begin{array}{c}\text{Larry}\\\text{He}\end{array}$ had a new bike.

3. Barbara gave her sister a rabbit. $\begin{array}{c}\text{Her sister}\\\text{She}\end{array}$ loved rabbits.

4. Mr. Ross and Mr. Long were teachers. $\begin{array}{c}\text{Mr. Ross}\\\text{He}\end{array}$ taught math.

5. Bill went fishing with Linda. $\begin{array}{c}\text{Linda}\\\text{She}\end{array}$ caught four fish.

6. Ann and her mother went to a party. $\begin{array}{c}\text{Ann}\\\text{She}\end{array}$ carried a cake.

Part B

1. six <u>chairs</u>

2. my fathers <u>chairs</u>

3. my fathers <u>chair</u>

4. some <u>apples</u>

5. that trees <u>leaves</u>

6. a cars <u>headlights</u>

7. a boys <u>kites</u>

8. two big <u>oranges</u>

9. those red <u>cars</u>

10. that boys <u>books</u>

11. the teachers <u>pencil</u>

12. the tallest <u>girls</u>

Part C   Circle each word that is a verb.

bought   smiled   green   tall   kicked   went   boy

Part A

1. Wendy and Debbie went to the beach. $\begin{matrix} \text{Wendy} \\ \text{She} \end{matrix}$ flew her kite.

2. Robert and Dave walked home. $\begin{matrix} \text{Dave} \\ \text{He} \end{matrix}$ carried a radio.

3. Tom and Pam walked to school. $\begin{matrix} \text{Pam} \\ \text{She} \end{matrix}$ liked to walk fast.

4. Ed and Sam talked in the hall. $\begin{matrix} \text{Ed} \\ \text{He} \end{matrix}$ stood near the door.

5. Linda helped Alice build a table. $\begin{matrix} \text{Linda} \\ \text{She} \end{matrix}$ wanted to paint it red.

6. Ed asked Bob about school. $\begin{matrix} \text{Ed} \\ \text{He} \end{matrix}$ had been absent for a week.

Part B

1. a girls <u>hairbrush</u>

2. that cats <u>tail</u>

3. the birds in the <u>tree</u>

4. the bugs on the <u>table</u>

5. those cats near <u>John</u>

6. an old mans <u>face</u>

7. the womans <u>umbrella</u>

8. many <u>cups</u>

9. a girls <u>suitcase</u>

Part A

1. Bill and Frank ate lunch. ~~He~~ Bill had a peanut butter sandwich.

2. Miss Winston and Miss Kelly were teachers. ~~She~~ Miss Kelly taught reading.

3. Kevin told Ann about a movie. ~~He~~ Kevin thought it was very funny.

4. My father gave Betty a book. ~~She~~ Betty liked to read books about space.

5. Tina sat next to Jane. ~~She~~ Tina was the smartest girl in class.

6. Wendy worked with Bill. ~~She~~ Wendy fixed a flat tire.

Part B   Change each sentence so the subject is a pronoun. Cross out the subject. Write the pronoun above it.

1. The old man could not start the car.

2. A storm lasted all night.

3. A dog and a cow were eating.

4. The young woman cleaned a table.

5. The trucks went up the hill.

6. A mother held a baby.

Lesson 55

Part A   Circle the subject in each sentence.
Write **P** in front of every sentence that has a pronoun for a subject.

___ 1. Donald planted corn.

___ 2. It had a broken handle.

___ 3. He kicked a football.

___ 4. Betty baked three pies.

___ 5. The truck had 16 wheels.

___ 6. They woke up late.

___ 7. She planted corn.

___ 8. Bugs ran all over the table.

Part B

_____ and _____ were swimming. _____ wore a bathing cap. _____ also wore a watch.

_____ sat near the water.

_____ wore sunglasses.

_____ stood next to the blanket.

_____ wore shorts. _____ read a book.

Part C

1. the boys goed to Bills house. (3)

2. Alice fell asleep she was very tired. (2)

3. that boys shirt has six red buttons and four yellow buttons (3)

4. My best friends are jerry gomez and alex jordan. (4)

5. Melissa and richard put their dog on richards bed. (3)

6. We looked outside and The rain had just stopped. (2)

Lesson 56

Part A   Circle the subject in each sentence.
Write **P** in front of each sentence that has a pronoun for a subject.

___ 1. The tree was beautiful.

___ 2. He ate pizza for dinner.

___ 3. Those dogs chased our cat.

___ 4. Tina read a book.

___ 5. It fell off the table.

___ 6. They bought new shirts.

___ 7. My sister painted the room.

___ 8. Robert finished his homework.

Part B

_____ and _____ picked apples from a tree.

_____ wore a hat. _____ had a beard. _____ stood on

a box. _____ held a bucket. _____ and _____ sat on a

blanket. _____ read a book. _____ wore a shirt with the

number 9 on the back. _____ drew a picture.

Part C

1. My dads cat had four kittens   (2)

2. She teached robert and jerry how to ride a bike.   (3)

3. she washed the windows of her dads car   (3)

4. We seen mrs. jordan in the store she waved to us.   (5)

70

Part A   Circle the subject in each sentence.
Write **P** in front of each sentence that has a pronoun for a subject.

____ 1. Linda's shirt was dirty.

____ 2. They painted the door.

____ 3. He is ten years old.

____ 4. A new girl walked into our class.

____ 5. It had big tires.

____ 6. A boy and his friend went to the store.

____ 7. My little brother is seven years old.

____ 8. She walked to school.

Part B

_____ and _____ were playing basketball.

_____ bounced a ball. _____ wore shorts and long socks.

_____ wore a headband to keep her hair from getting in her eyes.

_____ jumped into the air as she shot the ball toward the basket.

_____ leaned against a pole as she watched the girls play basketball.

_____ read a newspaper. _____ sat on a bench.

Part A

1. Ann walked to school with Jenny. A car splashed water on Ann.
    her.

2. Randy and Steve ran down the street. A black cat ran in front of Steve.
    him.

3. Tom saw Nancy at the store. The clerk was giving Nancy change.
    her

4. Frank talked to Peter. Everybody liked Peter.
    him.

5. Beth went swimming with Mike. She splashed water at Mike.
    him.

Part B

1. He went to the store <u>after dinner</u>.

2. She fell asleep <u>before the movie ended</u>.

3. A bird started to sing <u>early in the morning</u>.

4. The boy cleaned the garage after breakfast.

5. Ann fixed her car yesterday.

6. All the people clapped when the movie ended.

Lesson 59

Part A

1. Don and Mark raked leaves. Carol gave $\genfrac{}{}{0pt}{}{\text{Don}}{\text{him}}$ a bag for the leaves.

2. Mr. Swift fixed lunch for Miss Adams. He gave $\genfrac{}{}{0pt}{}{\text{Miss Adams}}{\text{her}}$ a large bowl of soup.

3. Linda wanted to be a clown for Halloween. Steve found a funny outfit for $\genfrac{}{}{0pt}{}{\text{Linda}}{\text{her}}$ to wear.

4. Tina and Alice waited in the doctor's office. The nurse told $\genfrac{}{}{0pt}{}{\text{Alice}}{\text{her}}$ to go into the room.

5. Jeff and Kurt left school. Mr. Dukes gave $\genfrac{}{}{0pt}{}{\text{Kurt}}{\text{him}}$ a ride home.

Part B

1. Two trees fell down during the storm.

2. The baby started to cry when his mother left the room.

3. Tom finished his homework at eleven o'clock in the morning.

4. The boy cleaned his room while his mother went shopping.

5. They shook hands after the game.

6. We went to the movies last night.

Part A

1. He brushed his teeth after he washed his face.

2. James and Tom did their math in the morning.

3. The engine made a funny noise before the car stopped.

4. Tom read a book while he waited for his brother.

5. Alice and her mother went shopping yesterday afternoon.

6. Our teacher read a story during the lunch hour.

7. The clown climbed the rope when a bell rang.

8. Smoke came from the house after lightning hit it.

Part B Write each sentence with the correct punctuation.
Make sure you follow these punctuation rules:
a. Put a comma after the word **said.**
b. Capitalize the first word the person said.
c. Put a period or a question mark after the last word the person said.
d. Put quote marks around the exact words the person said.

1.	She said why are you so happy
2.	He said the sun is shining
3.	Tim said do you have a pencil
4.	Alice said my pencil is broken

Part A

1. Our dog barked when the door opened.

2. We went shopping last night.

3. The girls painted the room while the boys washed the car.

4. Everybody fell asleep after lunch.

5. He held his nose as he jumped into the water.

6. Nobody talked during the movie.

Part B   Write **V** above each **verb.** Write **P** above each **pronoun.**

1. <u>It</u> <u>was landing</u> on the runway.
     1   2

2. <u>They</u> wheeled <u>it</u> into the store.
     3   4

3. The dog <u>barked</u> loudly at <u>him</u>.
         5   6

4. <u>He</u> <u>forgot</u> his homework.
     7 8

Part A

1. John went home after the party.
2. After the party, John went home.

3. The girls were tired by the time the sun went down.
4. By the time the sun went down, the girls were tired.

5. The engine made a funny noise before the car stopped.
6. Before the car stopped, the engine made a funny noise.

7. Tammy listened to the radio while Bill did his homework.
8. While Bill did his homework, Tammy listened to the radio.

Part B

1. Tom said, "why did you do that?   (2)

2. They seen fred and jerry at the store.   (3)

3. Maria said "i love math."   (2)

4. Lisa teached Marys brother to swim.   (2)

5. My sister went to the doctor and she had a cold.   (3)

Lesson 63

Part A

| Part A | Circle the subject. Underline the whole predicate. Make a line over the part that tells when. |

1. Jane got a lot of work done while the baby slept.

   While the baby slept, Jane got a lot of work done.

2. The birds flew south in September.

   In September, the birds flew south.

3. She woke up before the alarm clock rang.

   Before the alarm clock rang, she woke up.

4. He worked on his boat every night.

   Every night, he worked on his boat.

Part B

1. The dogs chased the cats. I watched   the cats / them   climb up a tree.

2. The boys and girls cleaned the house.   The boys / They   washed the windows.

3. The rabbits ran under the fence.   The rabbits / They   wanted the carrots.

4. Linda spoke to the boys. She told   the boys / them   about the test.

5. He washed the forks and spoons. He put   the forks / them   on the table.

77

Part A

1. Jane walked home after school.

   After school Jane walked home.

2. Tom read a book in the evening.

   In the evening Tom read a book.

3. The girl rubbed her eyes when the lights came on.

   When the lights came on the girl rubbed her eyes.

Part B

1. Sally had pencils and pens. She gave   the pens   to her friend.
                                            them

2. Tony found two kittens. He gave   the kittens   some milk.
                                       them

3. We saw bears and elephants.   The elephants   were eating peanuts.
                                    They

4. The boys and girls played baseball.   The girls   won the game.
                                           They

Part C

1. They said we are hungry.   (4)

2. She teached jerry to cook.   (2)

3. I said "are you tired?   (3)

4. The bus went up the hill it made lots of noise.   (2)

5. Jeff made dinner and he made a pie for dessert   (4)

Part A   Write **N** above the noun in each subject.

1. Dark clouds covered the sky.

2. An old dog slept on the floor.

3. The trucks got dirty.

4. Her little bike cost a lot of money.

5. My sister walked to school.

Part B

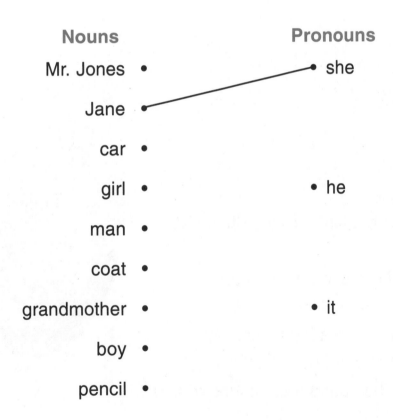

Nouns	Pronouns
Mr. Jones	she
Jane	
car	
girl	he
man	
coat	
grandmother	it
boy	
pencil	

Part A

girl •   • it

truck •

Tom •

apple •   • her

sister •

uncle •

Linda •   • him

light •

boy •

Part B

_____ 1. He fell asleep on the floor.

_____ 2. A big bird flew into the nest.

_____ 3. Alice came home early.

_____ 4. It made a big noise.

_____ 5. The young man started to speak.

_____ 6. Those girls are my sisters.

Part A

_____ 1. A broken bottle was on the floor.

_____ 2. It cost too much.

_____ 3. She is older than her sister.

_____ 4. That invention was very helpful.

_____ 5. Frogs make funny noises.

_____ 6. They are sleeping.

Part B

1. James said, Today is my birthday. We are having a party. (2)

2. Bill met Alice in the park. She said you look good. (4)

3. Anns dad is very tall he plays basketball. (3)

4. The doctor said you have a bad cold. Don't go outside. (4)

5. I seen ann and jane at Mr. jordans house. (5)

Lesson 68

Part A Write **N** above each noun.
Write **P** above each pronoun.
Write **V** above each verb.

1. Six rabbits played on it.

2. Tom looked at them.

3. They talked to him after lunch.

4. The meeting made her mad.

5. She saw it when she came home.

6. A big dog was with her.

Part B Put in the correct ending mark.

1. When did you go home

2. You can go to the movies

3. Did you find your hat

4. My brother is sick

5. That dog is mean

6. Can you come with us

7. Is your dog in the house

Part C

1. He said I can't find my dog. Have you seen him? (3)

2. She can drive a car and her brother taught her to drive. (3)

3. Linda adams and chris jordan were in my class (4)

4. James said, "where is Toms shirt? He wants it back. (3)

5. My brother was sick he had a bad cold. (2)

Lesson 69

Part A

1. The boys went home after school.

2. During the rainstorm our dog hid under the bed.

3. After we fixed the car we made dinner.

4. In the morning Jane walked to school.

5. That girl was happy when she got her report card.

6. He fell asleep while he read a book.

7. After James sat down the music started.

Part B   Put in the correct ending mark.

1. Where is Tom

2. Tom and Sally went home

3. Did you see that bird

4. Can he eat that big hamburger

5. A bird flew into the room

6. Is your brother here

7. She did not see her friend

Part C   Write **N** above each noun.
Write **P** above each pronoun.
Write **V** above each verb.

1. She stood next to him.

2. That girl gave him a book.

3. James saw her through that window.

4. Our cat played with them.

5. They were on top of it.

Part A Write **N** above each noun.
Write **P** above each pronoun.
Write **V** above each verb.

1. That new boy sat next to him.

2. Linda and her friend fixed it.

3. She took them to the park.

4. Six cows walked behind her.

Part B Rewrite each sentence so it begins with the part that tells when.

1. She fixed her car in the morning.

_____

_____

2. He went to sleep after he brushed his teeth.

_____

_____

3. The baby woke up when the bell rang.

_____

_____

4. Nobody talked during the movie.

_____

_____

Part C The number after each item tells how many mistakes are in the item. Fix up the mistakes.

1. Marias dog chased two cats up a tree (2)

2. The babies fell asleep on anns bed. (2)

3. Mr. adams said "I liked that book. (3)

4. Ann met Lindas brother he was very tall. (3)

5. He said my team won the game. (4)

Part D For each picture, write the sentences that tell the exact words the person said.

1. Hiro — Can you help me? My dog is lost.

2. Heather — That was fun. I had a good time.

1.	
2.	

Part A Put commas in the sentences that begin with the part that tells when.

1. A cat jumped up when the alarm clock rang.

2. When we got home the dog started barking.

3. In the morning we ate breakfast.

4. While the baby slept we talked quietly.

5. Her brother was happy when he got the letter.

6. They finished the job just before midnight.

7. Before they made lunch the cooks washed their hands.

Part B For each sentence, fill in the blank with the word **asked** or the word **said.** Then make the correct ending mark.

1. The girl _____, "Will you go with us "

2. The girl _____, "I want to go with you "

3. My friend _____, "I love baseball "

4. My friend _____, "Do you like baseball "

5. Ken _____, "Is it snowing "

6. Ken _____, "The snow is two feet deep "

Part C Write **N** in front of each noun.

1. _____ girl

2. _____ men

3. _____ they

4. _____ us

5. _____ yellow

6. _____ phone

7. _____ happy

8. _____ me

9. _____ mud

Lesson 72

Part A Write **N** above each noun.
Write **P** above each pronoun.
Write **V** above each verb.

1. They were on top of it.

2. A big dog followed them up the hill.

3. She gave him the ball.

4. Jerry was next to her.

Part B Write **N** in front of each noun.

1. _____ pen
2. _____ us
3. _____ flag
4. _____ under

5. _____ song
6. _____ them
7. _____ her
8. _____ found

9. _____ clouds
10. _____ school
11. _____ puppies
12. _____ party

Part C For each sentence, fill in the blank with the word **asked** or the word **said.** Then make the correct ending mark.

1. He _____, "Why are you so sad   "

2. She _____, "He has my book   "

3. His friend _____, "Where is the game   "

4. My sister _____, "Can we have a cookie   "

Part A

1. She bought a new car.

2. They went to a crowded beach.

3. Sam cooked dinner for them.

4. My truck ran over it.

Part B   For each sentence, fill in the blank with the word **asked** or the word **said.** Then make the correct ending mark.

1. He _____, "Is your brother home   "

2. He _____, "We had a good time   "

3. She _____, "My friend went home   "

4. She _____, "Where is the dog   "

Part C   Copy the paragraph. Change three sentences so they begin with the part that tells when.

Tom got up early in the morning. He ate breakfast after he put on warm clothes. Carol and her mother came over to Tom's house at 9 o'clock. They took Tom to a mountain. It was covered with snow. Tom and Carol threw snowballs when they got to the mountain top.

Lesson 74

Part A Punctuate the sentences that tell the exact words a person said. Put in the missing commas, quote marks and capital letters.

Jerry called Tom on the phone. Jerry asked Tom can you go to the movies?

Tom asked his mother can I go to the movies?

His mother said you can go when you finish your homework.

Tom finished his homework quickly. Tom's mom took Jerry and Tom to the movies later that day.

Write **N** above each noun.
Write **P** above each pronoun.
Write **V** above each verb.

1. The wind blew water at them.

2. My brother put salt on it.

3. She wanted a new bike last summer.

4. That old man sold it to me.

Part C

1. At midnight. The dog began to bark.   (2)

2. The streets flooded, during the rain storm   (2)

3. She bought a book. Before the store closed.   (2)

4. While the wind blew. Everybody stayed inside Toms house.   (3)

5. Ann fell asleep while toms dad sang.   (2)

6. Two old trees fell down, last night.   (1)

7. Before Anns dad made breakfast we washed our hands.   (2)

Lesson 75

Part A   Write **N** above each noun.
Write **P** above each pronoun.
Write **V** above each verb.

1. He threw it at the wall.

2. Tim and Donna were mad at them.

3. The dogs and cats ran after me.

4. Her arm had a bug on it.

Part B   Fix up any mistakes in each item.

1. When alice got to school. Nobody was there.   (3)

2. Jerry asked his mother can I stay home?"   (3)

3. Tom asked his sister where is my shirt   (5)

4. My sister wasn't home. She went to alices house.   (2)

5. As mr. jordan left. The children waved to him.   (4)

6. Bill cleaned his room, before he ate breakfast   (2)

Part A

> Write **N** above each noun.
> Write **P** above each pronoun.
> Write **V** above each verb.

1. A girl and her dog chased it around the park.

2. He was between a little desk and a big table.

3. Yesterday morning, she ate eggs and toast for breakfast.

4. In the morning, they took him to see me.

Part B

A.   B.   C.   D.

1. The boy was tall. _____

2. The boy was tall. He wore shorts. _____

3. The boy was tall. He wore shorts. He held a bat. _____

Part A

1. Ted and <u>Hilda</u> <u>were</u> on the <u>bank</u> of a <u>stream</u>.

2. When the <u>sun</u> came up, Ginger and <u>Tom</u> <u>walked</u> to the <u>barn</u>.

3. Before <u>school</u>, the little <u>boy</u> <u>looked</u> for <u>them</u>.

4. <u>She</u> <u>felt</u> tired after the <u>party</u>.

Part B

> **Rule:** If you remove the word **and,** you must replace it with a comma.

1. Ann had fun swimming <u>and</u> playing ball and digging in the sand.

2. Girls <u>and</u> boys <u>and</u> dogs and cats slid down the hill.

3. James read a book and wrote two letters and called his uncle and cleaned his room.

4. A cat and a dog and a pig and a horse ran into the barn.

Part C

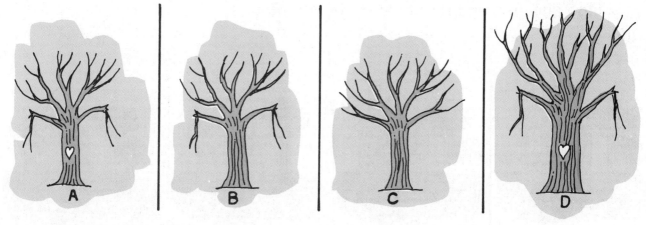

1. The tree was small. _____

2. The tree was small. It had broken branches. _____

3. The tree was small. It had broken branches. It had a heart carved on it. _____

Part A

1. A <u>dog</u> and a <u>cat</u> <u>were</u> next to <u>her</u>.

2. After the <u>rain</u> <u>stopped</u>, <u>they</u> went to his <u>house</u>.

3. <u>She</u> <u>put</u> <u>apples</u> and <u>oranges</u> in her bag.

4. Yesterday <u>morning</u>, their <u>mother</u> <u>drove</u> <u>them</u> to school.

Part B

- If there are two **ands,** cross out the first **and.** Replace it with a comma.
- If there is only one **and,** leave it.

1. Tom ate chicken and peas and carrots.
2. Jane jumped rope and climbed on the bars and walked on her hands.
3. Jerry jumped up and ran to the door.
4. A book and a pencil and a cup fell off the table.
5. Alice opened the door and got into the car and drove to work.
6. James and his sister went home.
7. Jane and Tom and Bill ate lunch under the tree.

Part C

1. The house had two trees next to it. It had broken windows. _____
2. The house had two trees next to it. It had broken windows. It had a chimney. _____
3. The house had two trees next to it. _____

Part A
- If there are two **ands,** cross out the first **and.** Replace it with a comma.
- If there is only one **and,** leave it.

1. Jerry got into the car and turned on the engine and drove home.

2. Mary and Jim and Tom were sick yesterday.

3. James ate a piece of bread and drank a glass of milk.

4. Bill wore black shoes and a red shirt and brown pants.

5. A cat and a dog and a pig lived in the barn.

6. My mother and my little sister walked to the store.

7. Walter washed the windows and made his bed and swept the floor.

Part B   Fix up any mistakes in each item.

1. Bill asked his mother when will we eat dinner   (5)

2. When the dog barked at a cat. The baby woke up.   (2)

3. Tom brushed his teeth, after he washed his face   (2)

4. Abdul said, "I am hungry. I want an apple   (2)

5. The boys cleaned their teachers desk.   (1)

6. Where is mr. suzuki   (3)

Lesson 80 – Test 8

Test Score ____

Part A

Part A   Write **N** above each noun.
Write **P** above each pronoun.
Write **V** above each verb.

1. My sister found them in her coat.

2. In the morning, he wrote a letter.

3. Yesterday afternoon, they saw a movie about Texas.

4. She walked in the street with her dog.

Part B   For each sentence, circle the subject and underline the whole predicate.

1. My sister and I went home on the bus.

2. After the sun went down, the sky became cloudy.

3. While the baby slept, everybody whispered.

4. Those birds will fly away when they finish eating.

5. In the evening, James read a book.

Part C For each sentence, fill in the blank with the word **asked** or the word **said.** Then make the correct ending mark.

1. James _____, "Can you help me "

2. They _____, "We won the game "

3. She _____, "My dog's name is Rover "

4. He _____, "What is your dog's name "

Part D Put a comma in each sentence that begins with the part that tells when.

1. While the wind blew everybody stayed inside.

2. My sister got home before I did.

3. After the rain stopped my friends and I walked home.

4. As she walked home Julie listened to the music.

5. An old tree fell down during the storm.

6. Before our dad made breakfast we cleaned our room.

7. All the cars stopped when the light turned red.

Lesson

Part A   Complete each sentence with the verb **was** or the verb **were.**

1. Those girls _____ happy.

2. Girls and boys _____ hungry.

3. A baby _____ sleepy.

4. Five dogs _____ chasing a cat.

5. Those three books _____ new.

6. My mother _____ next to the car.

7. He _____ at the park.

8. They _____ late for school.

Part B

1. She had more stickers than James had.

2. Yesterday afternoon, they cleaned their room.

3. When the sun came up, Alice called him.

4. My sister gave me a new shirt.

Part C   Fix up the sentences that have too many **ands.**

1. They bought three apples and six oranges.
2. His sister bought five apples and two oranges and three carrots.
3. Raymond and Ned talked quietly.
4. Alice and Julio and Clark talked quietly.
5. We cleaned our room and ate dinner and did our homework before we
   went to sleep.

Lesson

Complete each sentence with the verb **was** or the verb **were.**

1. My father _____ sick.

2. Her older brothers _____ behind the car.

3. They _____ eating dinner.

4. Two horses _____ in the barn.

5. I _____ walking my dog.

6. Their dad _____ eating lunch.

7. My mother and father _____ happy.

Part B

1. Last winter, they went to see their grandmother.

2. It was next to the big bottle.

3. After they ate, she played with the baby.

4. Linda and James sat near me.

Part C   Use your lined paper. Rewrite each sentence so the word **and** appears only once.

1. The boy ran and slipped on the ice and fell down.

2. John and Mary and Jim went jogging.

3. They were tired and thirsty and hungry.

Part A Complete each sentence with the verb **was** or the verb **were.**

1. Jenny and John _____ reading.

2. That pencil _____ sharp.

3. Five fish _____ swimming in the tank.

4. Terry _____ fishing from the boat.

5. An old woman _____ tired.

6. They _____ playing football.

Part B Fix up any mistakes in each item.

1. Alice asked, "where is my car   (3)

2. After mr. adams ate. he went home.   (3)

3. James asked his mother can I go out to play?"   (3)

4. Alice sat down, when she finished the race.   (1)

5. Two birds flew over anns head   (3)

Part A	Complete each sentence with the verb **was** or the verb **were**.

1. You _____ right.

2. You _____ late yesterday.

3. She _____ sad.

4. You _____ not home yesterday.

5. He _____ late.

6. They _____ sick.

7. His dog _____ friendly.

8. You _____ hiding.

Part B

1. Write a description about picture 1. Tell where the women were and what they were doing.

2. Write a description about picture 2. Tell where the women were and what they were doing.

Lesson 86

Part A

1. Suddenly, a big <u>wind</u> <u>knocked</u> <u>him</u> off the <u>chair</u>.

2. He <u>put</u> a <u>cow</u> and a <u>pig</u> in the old red <u>barn</u>.

3. After <u>lunch</u>, my <u>mother</u> took <u>me</u> to the swimming <u>pool</u>.

4. A <u>snowball</u> <u>landed</u> next to <u>her</u>.

Part B — For each noun, write **day, month** or **name.**

1. Jay Turner _____

2. October _____

3. Wednesday _____

4. Friday _____

5. David _____

6. December _____

Part C

1. Make up a sentence that tells who **went into the store.**

2. Make up a sentence that tells which animals **stood on a diving board.**

3. Make up a sentence that tells the things **the woman juggled.**

Lesson

Part A

Pronouns	Names	Pronouns

Pronouns   Names   Pronouns

• Sue and Alice •

I •   • Mrs. Jones •   • we

• Tom and Jill •

me •   • Sam •   • us

• Mary •

• Ted, Ned and Fred •

Part B

1. After the <u>rain</u> stopped, <u>we</u> <u>walked</u> to <u>school</u>.

2. Last night, <u>I</u> <u>helped</u> <u>him</u> do his <u>homework</u>.

3. The <u>airplane</u> <u>took</u> <u>her</u> to <u>Texas</u>.

4. <u>She</u> <u>taught</u> <u>me</u> how to fix <u>bikes</u>.

Part A

Pronouns	Names	Pronouns
	• Mr. Alvirez •	
I •	• Alice and Jane •	• we
	• Bryan, Tim and Robin •	
me •	• Jason •	• us
	• Chris and James •	
	• Debbie •	

Part B   Fix up the mistakes in each item.

1. Tom and I was both born on the first wednesday in december.   (3)

2. Janes hand got dirty, when she planted trees   (3)

3. Ann visited her grandmother every monday night in april and

   may.   (3)

4. Cats and dogs was running in Toms yard.   (2)

5. Alex and i were talking to cora.   (2)

6. Kay asked her dad can i stay up late?   (5)

7. When mr. adams got home on Thursday. He read the

   newspaper.   (4)

Lesson 89

Part A

1. At last, my <u>brother</u> and <u>I</u> finished our <u>homework</u>.

2. Yesterday, <u>we</u> <u>helped</u> <u>Mary</u> fix her <u>car</u>.

3. <u>Alice</u> and her <u>sister</u> <u>were</u> not with <u>me</u>.

4. Her <u>car</u> <u>had</u> a racing <u>stripe</u>.

Part B   **Fix up the mistakes in each item.**

1. Mr. Adams and mrs. sanchez was sick on wednesday. (4)

2. Jill asked Tom can i help you?" (4)

3. When my mom walked into the room. My baby sister smiled. (2)

4. Where did you put Jills coat (2)

5. You was born in february. (2)

6. She asked was he born in september or october?" (5)

Part A

1. After the <u>rain</u> stopped, Alice and <u>I</u> <u>walked</u> home.

2. <u>We</u> <u>played</u> <u>basketball</u> with a tall <u>man</u>.

3. My <u>friend</u> <u>was</u> next to <u>me</u>.

4. After we <u>ate</u> lunch, <u>Bob</u> showed <u>us</u> how to fly <u>kites</u>.

Part B

1. Make up a sentence that tells who chased the squirrel.
2. Make up a sentence that tells what Raymond was holding.

Lesson 91

Part A

1. Last night, <u>we</u> <u>ate</u> dinner in a <u>restaurant</u>.

2. Her big <u>sister</u> <u>was</u> not with <u>them</u>.

3. <u>I</u> <u>called</u> <u>her</u> this <u>morning</u>.

4. When the <u>rain</u> stopped, <u>Liz</u> and <u>Alex</u> <u>walked</u> home.

Part B

> **Rule:** Any word that comes before the noun in the subject is an adjective.

       N

1. (A little puppy) is barking.

      N

2. (Nine boys) ate lunch.

                    N

3. (A beautiful red kite) flew in the air.

Part C

For each sentence, circle the subject.
- Write **N** above the noun in the subject.
- Write **A** above each adjective in the subject.

1. An old tree grew next to the house.

2. That farmer had big hands.

3. Six little black cats ran in front of me.

4. Small clouds moved across the sky.

5. Those happy boys cheered loudly.

6. The dog was hungry.

Part A

1. His brother bought a new hat.

2. My sister baked a yellow cake.

3. Five red ants climbed the kitchen wall.

4. An old red cup fell off the big table.

Part B   **Fix up the mistakes in each sentence.**

1. Jerry asked, "can Raymond and i go to the movies   (4)

2. My dads hand is twice as big as Jerrys hand.   (2)

3. When the baby fell asleep. Everybody was happy.   (2)

4. Alice Chuck and ellen ate lunch at Ellens house.   (3)

5. December january and february was cold months.   (4)

6. Alice was very tired, when she got home on monday.   (2)

Part A
- Write **N** above each noun.
- Write **A** above each adjective.

1. One man held a big net.

2. Her children bought ten cookies.

3. The gray squirrel climbed a tall tree.

4. Two children washed their little dog.

Part B   Cross out the letters of the sentences that are **not** relevant to the question.

How is wood used?

ⓐ Wood is used for building things. ⓑ Wood is also used for fuel. ⓒ Some houses have walls that are made of wood. ⓓ Other houses are made of brick. ⓔ The floors of many houses are made of wood. ⓕ Some houses have floors made of concrete. ⓖ Concrete floors may crack when the house gets old. ⓗ Some window frames are made of wood. ⓘ Fine tables and chairs are made of wood. ⓙ Other chairs are made of metal or plastic.

Part A Write adjectives that make each subject complete.

1. _____ rabbit

2. _____ men

3. _____ cup

4. _____ monster

Part B

1. Suddenly, <u>he</u> <u>jumped</u> out of <u>bed</u>.

2. Nine <u>men</u> <u>helped</u> <u>me</u> fix my <u>car</u>.

3. <u>Dan</u> and his <u>sister</u> <u>were</u> with <u>us</u>.

4. After <u>we</u> <u>ate</u>, my <u>mother</u> was tired.

Lesson 97

Part A   Capitalize all parts of any item that names one person or one place.

1. that boy

2. tom

3. mrs. robert brown

4. my teacher

5. lincoln street

6. a repair shop

7. johnson repair shop

8. chicago, illinois

9. mississippi river

10. my store

11. jolly time toy store

12. that river

Part B   Cross out the letters of the sentences that are **not** relevant to the question.

> **What did Bob and Sally do when they saw a burning house?**

(a) Bob and Sally ran into the house when they saw smoke coming from the house. (b) While Bob filled a pail with water, Sally grabbed the fire extinguisher. (c) Bob and Sally worked in the same factory. (d) They saw that a chair and a table were on fire. (e) Bob threw water on the chair while Sally squirted the fire extinguisher on the table. (f) That night, Bob and Sally watched television.

Part C   • Write **N** above each noun.
• Write **A** above each adjective.

1. Three sad clowns rode a tiny bicycle.

2. Kathy is sleeping on the couch.

3. A striped kite hit the tree.

4. A cow ate grass.

5. Ten plates broke when they hit the floor.

Lesson 98

Part A   Capitalize all parts of any item that names one person or one place.

1. uncle jake

2. the street

3. san francisco

4. kennedy high school

5. our uncle

6. ace toy factory

7. united states

8. the mail carrier

9. pacific ocean

10. a big country

11. japan

12. adams street

Part B   • Write **N** above each noun.
• Write **A** above each adjective.

1. His bear juggled three balls.

2. A sick boy sat in a wheelchair.

3. Al ate two apples.

4. That woman held a small red purse.

5. Three people fixed that old red car.

Lesson 99

113

Part A Capitalize all parts of any item that names one person or one place.

1. ruth garcia

2. a doctor

3. a big building

4. fairview hospital

5. don's supermarket

6. dr. brown

7. that avenue

8. salt lake city

9. mr. jordan

10. his street

11. florida

12. spring avenue

Part B

1. Seven men went to a big party.

2. Two little children stood in deep snow.

3. James was wearing striped shorts.

4. An old woman gave me a dollar.

Lesson 100 – Test 10

Part A Write **V** above each verb.
Write **N** above each noun.
Write **A** above each adjective.

1. Six new cars went up the steep hill.

2. A strong wind knocked over an old fence.

Part B Fix up each sentence so it is punctuated correctly.

1. Alice had a dog a cat and a bird.   (1)

2. Mr. James Mrs. James and their son ate breakfast.   (1)

3. We bought apples oranges and pears at the store.   (1)

Part C Capitalize all parts of any item that names one person or one place.

1. a big store
2. united states
3. dr. mitchell
4. california

5. washington avenue
6. her house
7. that river
8. ace toy store

Part D Fill in each blank with the verb **was** or **were.**

1. They _____ not home.

2. Jim's cat _____ sitting on the fence.

3. Anna and her mother _____ at the store.

4. You _____ right.

5. An old man _____ fishing.

6. You _____ not home last night.

Lesson  101

For each item, write the sentence that answers the question.

1. Question: What are cheetahs?

   Answer: The fastest land animals.

2. Question: Where do cheetahs live?

   Answer: In Africa.

3. Question: When do cheetahs hunt?

   Answer: During the day.

4. Question: How fast do cheetahs run?

   Answer: Over 60 miles an hour.

Part B

1. Five lions were in the cage.

2. A small airplane is landing now.

3. Steve was swimming in cold water.

4. The red ball bounced into a busy street.

Part C   Write an interesting passage on the topic.

	Why do I like summertime the best?

because   during   school   sometimes   evening

Lesson

For each item, write the sentence that answers the question.

1. Question: Where do the largest elephants live?

   Answer: In Africa.

2. Question: How long do some elephants live?

   Answer: More than 50 years.

3. Question: How much do some elephants weigh?

   Answer: Up to six tons.

Part B

1. When the bell rang, we went to our classroom.

2. Linda stood in front of a large desk.

3. That tiny black fly flew into my cup.

4. During the night, a strong wind blew.

Part A For each item, write the sentence that answers the question.

1. Question: Where do you find skunks?

   Answer: In North America.

2. Question: Why do skunks make a terrible smell?

   Answer: To defend themselves.

3. Question: When do skunks usually sleep?

   Answer: During the daytime.

4. Question: How do skunks show that they are angry?

   Answer: By raising their tails.

Part B

1. During the big storm, we went inside an old house.

2. He saw many black ants on the kitchen table.

3. Two old men helped her.

4. His truck moved slowly up a steep hill.

5. After the meeting, she went to the store.

Part A

1. I found four red marbles under that old rug.

2. Every day, we buy milk at the store.

3. An airplane flew over a big white cloud.

4. A bright light came from the third floor.

Part B

1. The mississippi river is the longest river in the united states.   (4)

2. Texas alaska and california are the biggest states.   (3)

3. Is los angeles bigger than san francisco?   (4)

4. We lived on baldwin street until last september.   (3)

5. After she brushed her teeth. She went to bed.   (2)

6. My favorite cities are new york dallas and miami.   (5)

7. Ann asked mr. james Where can i buy that book   (7)

Part A

1. Before the rain stopped.

_____

2. Stood on top of the table.

_____

3. She caught a bug.

_____

4. Mary sat down.

_____

5. Mary, Tom and their dog.

_____

6. After the show.

_____

Part B

1. After the storm, we had a fish in our basement.

2. His mother told us a funny story.

3. In my dream, five tigers were chasing me.

4. Tom and Fran ran over that hill.

Part A

1. After we finished eating.

_____

2. He opened it.

_____

3. A shirt, blue jeans and shoes.

_____

4. Before the snow stopped.

_____

5. She jumped up.

_____

Part B Write a good title sentence for each passage.

Passage 1

    Laurie put on her swimming suit. She jumped into the pool. She swam across the pool three times. Then she got out of the pool and dried off.

_____

Passage 2

    Ted made his bed. He picked up his dirty clothes from the bedroom floor. He put things in his closet. He swept the floor of his room. Then he cleaned the windows in his room.

_____

Part A	Write a good title sentence for each passage.

Passage 1

Kurt grabbed his dog and took it into the bathroom. He filled the bathtub with water. He put the dog in the tub. He rubbed soap on the dog. He rinsed off the dog.

_____

Passage 2

Brad took a can of cat food from the shelf. He opened the can. He put the cat food in a small dish. Then he put the dish on the floor. His cat ate all the food.

_____

Part B	For each sentence, circle the subject and underline the predicate.
	• Write **N** above each underlined noun.
	• Write **A** above each underlined adjective.
	• Write **V** above each underlined verb.
	• Write **P** above each underlined pronoun.

1. Fran and Ray ran to the beach.

2. In the evening, I saw big spiders on our front steps.

3. That old car runs like a new car.

4. He slipped on the icy stairs.

Part A	Write a good title sentence for each passage.

Passage 1

Steve took out some paper and a pen. He wrote on the paper. He put the paper in an envelope. He wrote his grandmother's name and address on the envelope. He put a stamp on the envelope.

_____

Passage 2

Melody put some paper in the fireplace. She put wood on top of the paper. She lit a match and held it under the paper. When the paper and wood started to burn, Melody closed the screen in front of the fireplace.

_____

Part B

1. The empire state building is in new york. (5)

2. Robert fed the dog washed the dishes and cleaned his room before lunch. (1)

3. Is mexico larger than canada (3)

4. Jill asked, "Where is Dr. Lees office? (2)

5. I bought apples oranges and pears at the store. (1)

6. December january and february are the coldest months of the year. (3)

7. Yokos sister lives on washington street. (3)

8. Tom and his sister was in the park. (1)

Part A

1. Before we went to sleep.

   _____

2. She helped him.

   _____

3. When they got home.

   _____

4. A truck, a car and a motorcycle.

   _____

5. He stopped talking.

   _____

Part B   For each sentence, circle the subject and underline the predicate.
* Write **N** above each underlined noun.
* Write **A** above each underlined adjective.
* Write **V** above each underlined verb.
* Write **P** above each underlined pronoun.

1. A large red truck stopped in front of them.

2. After school, six boys and two girls played in the gym.

3. She helped him fix the flat tire on his new bike.

Part A

1. In the morning, my older sister fixed breakfast for our family.

2. That old car stopped in front of a large building.

3. She was smiling when they went out the back door.

4. Two mean dogs were running after a yellow cat.

Part B

1. When she got home. everybody was sleeping. (1)

2. I live on madison avenue. (2)

3. The mississippi river is the longest river in the united states. (4)

4. Renee asked Alfred, "Have you seen my brother? He has my pen. (1)

5. Bills favorite team is the san francisco giants. (4)

6. June july and august are the warmest months. (3)

7. Does dr. spangler have an office on washington street (5)

Additional Practice

Test 1

Part A   Circle the part that names.   Underline the part that tells more.

1. They ate lunch in the park.
2. We saw three monkeys at the zoo.
3. A lion and a tiger were sleeping.
4. An old woman sat in front of me.
5. My brother and my sister were at school.
6. Their little dog barked all night.

Part B   Circle the part that names.   Underline the part that tells more.

1. My shirt and my pants were dirty.
2. A big truck went up the hill.
3. She fixed the broken window.
4. A man and a woman were in the car.
5. He walked to school.
6. Six red ants climbed onto the table.

Part C   Fix up the sentences so they tell what people did.

1. She is buying a shirt.

2. My teacher was giving me a book.

3. The dog is licking my face.

4. Her mother is finding the keys.

5. She was walking quickly.

6. They are spilling the water.

Fix up the sentences so they tell what people did.

1. Robin is starting her car.

2. Our class was having a party.

3. James is digging in the sand.

4. They were pushing the car.

5. Mr. Adams is finding his keys.

6. Alice was filling the glass.

Test 2

Part A **Put in capitals and periods. Circle the part of each sentence that names.**

mr. james cooked an apple pie he put the pie on the kitchen table a fly flew into the kitchen it landed on the apple pie mr. james got mad he swung a flyswatter at the fly he missed the fly he hit the pie the pie splattered all over the kitchen

Part B **Put in capitals and periods. Circle the part of each sentence that names.**

a little boy threw a ball the ball rolled into the street a big truck ran over the ball the boy started to cry the truck driver got out of the truck he bought a new ball for the boy

Part C

Robin and her little sister are going to the swimming pool. They are wearing their new bathing suits. They stayed at the pool all day. Robin is sitting in the sun. Her little sister is playing in the water.

Do the sentences tell what people did? **X X X X**

Part D

James is having a bad cold. He stayed home from school. He is wearing pajamas all day. He is sitting in front of the bedroom window. His mother is giving him hot soup.

Do the sentences tell what people did?   X   X   X   X

Part E   Fill in the blanks with **He, She** or **It.**

1. My father went swimming. _____ wore his new bathing suit.

2. His bike could go very fast. _____ had big tires.

3. My sister is eleven years old. _____ is in fifth grade.

Part F   Fill in the blanks with **He, She** or **It.**

1. Her brother was tired. _____ did not get enough sleep.

2. My grandmother called us. _____ asked us about school.

3. Her house is very big. _____ has four bedrooms.

Test 3

Part A   Circle the subject. Underline the predicate.

1. My sister was tired.
2. We tried to find it.
3. They flew away.
4. That little cat slept under the bed.
5. My teacher and his wife live near the school.
6. We saw Mr. Adams and his son.

Circle the subject. Underline the predicate.

1. They sat in a big old chair.
2. It stopped.
3. My red pencil fell off the table.

4. A cat and a dog chased the skunk.
5. Five striped cats played under the house.
6. A boy slept on the couch.

Part C Fix up the paragraph so each sentence begins with a capital and ends with a period.

A truck went up the hill. The truck went over a rock a big barrel fell out of the truck. the barrel rolled down the hill it crashed into a tree the barrel broke into little pieces.

Part D Fix up the paragraph so each sentence begins with a capital and ends with a period.

Bill's dog chased a butterfly. the butterfly flew away the dog ran through a big mud puddle. Bill took the dog into the bathroom he gave the dog a bath. the dog was not happy She wanted to play

Part E Fix up any sentences that should name **He, She** or **It**.

The children made a big sand castle at the beach. Robert made the walls. Robert used sand that was very wet. His sister made the towers. His sister worked very carefully. The sand castle was three feet high. The sand castle looked like something you would see in a book.

Linda had a birthday yesterday. Linda was eleven years old. Her father brought a cake to school. Her father gave cake to each student. The cake tasted great. The cake had chocolate and strawberry filling.

Test 4

Part A   Fix up each person's name so all parts of the name begin with a capital.

1. alan davis
2. mr. james
3. my teacher

4. a doctor
5. robert crosby
6. her sister

7. david tanaka
8. my best friend
9. david jackson

Part B   Fix up each person's name so all parts of the name begin with a capital.

1. mrs. jackson
2. two cowboys
3. paul adams

4. ronnie nolasco
5. my sister
6. that fire fighter

7. mrs. ray
8. michael walker
9. a football player

Part C   Fill in the blanks with **He, She, It** or **They.**

1. Her friends went home.

2. A dog and a cat chased the skunk.

3. Her brother came home early.

4. His toy was broken.

5. My sister drove the car.

6. The girls helped me.

1. _____ went home.

2. _____ chased the skunk.

3. _____ came home early.

4. _____ was broken.

5. _____ drove the car.

6. _____ helped me.

Part D Fill in the blanks with **He, She, It** or **They.**

1. That old truck went fast.
2. Apples cost 42 cents.
3. The men wore cowboy hats.
4. His mother talked on the phone.
5. Our car had a flat tire.
6. Her friends went home.

1. _____ went fast.
2. _____ cost 42 cents.
3. _____ wore cowboy hats.
4. _____ talked on the phone.
5. _____ had a flat tire.
6. _____ went home.

Part E Circle the subject. Underline the predicate.

1. Three horses and a cow were in the barn.
2. She fell asleep.
3. A little bird flew into the house.
4. It was very large.
5. A big glass was next to the plate.
6. They stopped suddenly.

Part F Circle the subject. Underline the predicate.

1. His dad went into the house.
2. He talked.
3. Two girls and a boy entered the room.
4. That friendly animal smiled at us.
5. It stopped.
6. Everybody started to talk.

Test 5

Read the paragraph. Fix up any run-ons.

Nancy Wilson and Jane Robinson lived in a big city and they wanted to visit a friend who lived on a farm. The girls worked every day after school to earn money for the trip and Nancy helped Mr. Jackson fix his car. Jane helped Mr. Baker paint his apartment and then Nancy and Jane soon had enough money for the trip.

Part B   Read the paragraph. Fix up any run-ons.

Yuri and Bill found a little bird that had fallen out of its nest and then they took the little bird home with them. Mr. Robinson gave them a book about birds and the book told how to take care of the bird. Yuri fed the bird while Bill made a bed for it and then the bird got better. Yuri and Bill took it back to its nest.

Part C   Write the verb for each sentence.

1. She stopped the car. _____

2. A young man was walking on the path. _____

3. That truck had a flat tire. _____

4. Linda and Sandy were eating apples. _____

5. Everybody clapped. _____

6. He sat near the door. _____

Write the verb for each sentence.

1. She painted her room. _____

2. They were sitting on the floor. _____

3. His shirt was not dirty. _____

4. He was helping his mother. _____

5. A cow and a horse ate the grass. _____

6. That nice woman helped us. _____

Part E Rewrite each item with an apostrophe **s.**

1. The car belonged to **my uncle.** The car had a flat tire.

_____ had a flat tire.

2. The cat belonged to **her friend.** The cat was sleeping.

_____ was sleeping.

3. The hat belonged to **Jill.** The hat was on the table.

_____ was on the table.

4. The toy belonged to **the baby.** The toy was broken.

_____was broken.

Part F Rewrite each item with an apostrophe **s.**

1. The book belonged to **Jean.** The book had two hundred pages.

_____ had two hundred pages.

2. The glasses belonged to **my sister.** The glasses were dirty.

_____ were dirty.

3. The shirt belonged to **the teacher.** The shirt had red and white stripes.

_____had red and white stripes.

4. The leg belonged to **Ray.** The leg was broken.

_____ was broken.

Part G Fill in the blanks with the correct words.

Three women were working.

_____ were building a house.

_____ sawed a board. _____

stood next to the house. _____

hammered nails into boards.

_____ carried three boards.

_____ had them on her shoulder.

Part H Fill in the blanks with the correct words.

_____ and _____

were working. _____ were doing

yard work. _____ sawed a

branch from a tree. _____ wore

a hat and work clothes. _____

held the branch with one hand.

_____ dug a hole in the dirt.

Test 7

Part A
Write **N** above each noun.
Write **P** above each pronoun.
Write **V** above each verb.

1. They talked to her.

2. A little cat sat next to him.

3. The rain made them sad.

4. He saw it.

Part B
Write **N** above each noun.
Write **P** above each pronoun.
Write **V** above each verb.

1. Linda helped him.

2. They were next to her.

3. My teacher saw it.

4. That new book helped them.

Part C
The number after each item tells how many mistakes are in the item.
Fix up the mistakes.

1. James said, Today is my birthday. We are having a party. (2)

2. Bill met Alice in the park. She said you look good. (4)

3. Anns dad is very tall he plays basketball. (3)

4. The doctor said you have a bad cold. Don't go outside. (4)

5. I saw ann and jane at Mr. jordans house. (4)

1. Mr. roberts said "That is his bike.   (3)

2. the boys went to Bills house.   (2)

3. that boys shirt has six red buttons and four yellow buttons   (3)

4. My best friends are jerry gomez and alex jordan.   (4)

5. Melissa and richard put their dog on richards bed.   (3)

6. He said I am hungry. I want an apple   (4)

Test 8

Part A | Write **N** above each underlined noun.
Write **P** above each underlined pronoun.
Write **V** above each underlined verb.

1. He bought a new shirt at the store.

2. Yesterday morning, we saw her.

3. My school had a big playground.

4. A girl painted her room.

Write **N** above each underlined noun.
Write **P** above each underlined pronoun.
Write **V** above each underlined verb.

1. She stood in front of the table.

2. In the morning, she ate an apple.

3. The water dripped on it.

4. After the party, she walked to her house.

Part C For each sentence, circle the subject and underline the whole predicate.

1. Before the sun went down, the birds began to sing.

2. Jason and Robert fell asleep after a few minutes.

3. After school, we walked home.

4. Last night, everybody went to sleep early.

5. We had eggs for breakfast.

Part D For each sentence, circle the subject and underline the whole predicate.

1. When the light turned green, she put her foot on the gas pedal.

2. After dinner, my dad took a nap.

3. He felt very tired when he got home.

4. Before school, we played on the bars.

5. My brother and my sister were at school.

For each sentence, fill in the blank with the word **asked** or the word **said.** Then make the correct ending mark.

1. Her friend _____, "That was a good meal "

2. Jane _____, "Did it rain "

3. He _____, "Are you hungry "

4. Jason _____, "Nobody is home "

Part F For each sentence, fill in the blank with the word **asked** or the word **said.** Then make the correct ending mark.

1. He _____, "Is lunch ready "

2. They _____, "Did you see her "

3. Alice _____, "Where is Adams Avenue "

4. He _____, "It's time to eat "

Part G Put a comma in each sentence that begins with the part that tells when.

1. The boys went home after school.

2. During the rainstorm our dog hid under the bed.

3. After we fixed the car we made dinner.

4. In the morning Jane walked to school.

5. That girl was happy when she got her report card.

6. He fell asleep while he read a book.

7. After James sat down the music started.

Put a comma in each sentence that begins with the part that tells when.

1. A cat jumped up when the alarm clock rang.

2. When we got home the dog started barking.

3. In the morning we ate breakfast.

4. While the baby slept we talked quietly.

5. Her brother was happy when he got the letter.

6. They finished the job just before midnight.

7. Before they made lunch the cooks washed their hands.

Test 10

Part A Write **V** above each verb.
Write **N** above each noun.
Write **A** above each adjective.

1. Four cats slept on the big pillow.

2. An old man drove a new car.

3. That smart girl knew every answer.

Part B Write **V** above each verb.
Write **N** above each noun.
Write **A** above each adjective.

1. A young boy jumped into the deep water.

2. Her uncle had a friendly dog.

3. Tom helped his little sister.

Part C   Fix up each sentence so it is punctuated correctly.

1. The flag was red white and blue. (1)

2. My brother my mother and my sister had colds. (1)

3. James opened the door put on his coat and walked down the stairs. (1)

Part D   Fix up each sentence so it is punctuated correctly.

1. We found two bottles three cans and six coins. (1)

2. Raymond his sister and Carmen went skating. (1)

3. Jean turned off the radio closed the window and turned on the heater. (1)

Part E   Capitalize all parts of any item that names one person or one place.

1. a big city   5. mississippi river

2. burnside avenue   6. dr. mitchell

3. bumpo car company   7. an old house

4. that lake   8. los angeles

Part F   Capitalize all parts of any item that names one person or one place.

1. my sister   5. this country

2. oak street   6. his street

3. new york   7. dr. evans

4. united states   8. delto stove company

Part G   Fill in each blank with the verb **was** or **were.**

1. Sandy and her mother _____ on the bus.

2. She _____ on the bus.

3. The girl's arm _____ sore.

4. You _____ wise to buy that book.

5. Three men _____ in the boat.

Part H   Fill in each blank with the verb **was** or **were.**

1. Ellen's son _____ sick.

2. You _____ wrong.

3. They _____ at school.

4. James and I _____ in the house.

5. The boy's teacher _____ happy.

6. You _____ first in line.

P.O. Box 10459
Eugene, Oregon 97440

Dear Student,

You'll do a lot of writing next year and for the rest of your life. You're off to a good start.

You know how to report.

You know how to interpret and figure out things that must have happened.

You know how to describe things to give the reader a clear picture.

You've also learned a lot about sentences and punctuation.

You know that a sentence has two parts—a subject and a predicate.

You know that you can say a sentence so it begins with the subject.

You know that the subject has a noun or a pronoun.

You know that the predicate usually begins with the verb.

You know that adjectives come before nouns and tell about the nouns.

You know that a sentence begins with a capital letter and ends with an ending mark.

You know how to capitalize nouns that name only one thing—one day of the week, one holiday, one building, one state or the name of one person.

You know that you make a comma to show where part of the predicate has been moved or to show that a word like **and** is missing.

And, most important, you know how to write. You know how to tell what people said, how to set the scene and how to tell what characters did when they solved a problem.

You're off to a good start. Remember all the things you've learned because you'll use them for the rest of your life.

Sincerely,

Zig Engelmann   Jerry Silbert